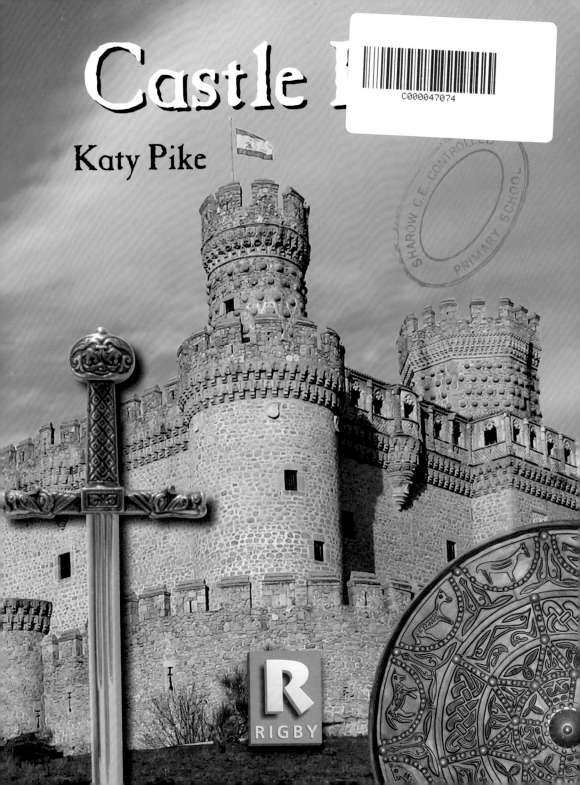

Castle

Katy Pike

R
RIGBY

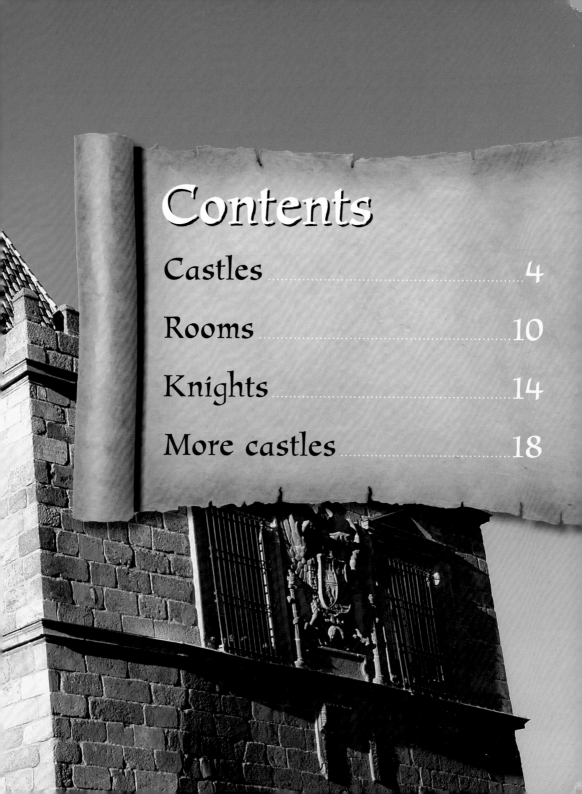

Contents

Castles

Castles are large houses.
They have very high walls.

Castles have very tall towers.

Castles have very large doors.

Some castles have
a deep moat.

Some castles have very large gardens.

Some castles have lots of windows.

Rooms

Castles have lots of rooms.

This is a sitting room
in a castle.

This is a bedroom
in a castle.

Castles have very
large kitchens.

This is the great hall
in a castle.

Castles have a
throne room.

Some castles have a large ballroom.

Castles have lots of stairs.

Knights

A knight lived in a castle.
A knight wore armour.

A knight wore gloves.
He wore a helmet, too.

15

A knight had a shield.
He had a long sword, too.

A knight rode a horse.

More castles

This castle is in England.

This is a map
of England.

England is on this large map, too.

This castle is in Spain.

This is a map of Spain.

Spain is on this large map, too.
Spain is near England.

This castle is in France.

This is a map of France.

Le Havre • ★PARIS • Nancy
Brest • • Le Mans • Dijon
F R A N C E
• Lyon
Clermont-Ferrand
Bordeaux •
Toulouse • Marseille

France is on this large map, too.
France is very near England.

Picture glossary

armour

castle

gloves

helmet

horse

knight

map

moat

shield

sword

throne

tower